Plan While You Can

Legal Solutions for Facing Disability

By

Roger W. Andersen

ISBN: 1-4107-6488-5 (e-book)
ISBN: 1-4107-6487-7 (Paperback)
ISBN: 1-4107-6486-9 (Dust Jacket)

Library of Congress Control Number: 2003094044

This book is printed on acid free paper.

Printed in the United States of America
Bloomington, IN

1stBooks – rev. 07/10/03

Other Books by Roger W. Andersen

Understanding Trusts and Estates

Fundamentals of Trusts and Estates

(with Ira Mark Bloom)

To Butch and Mike

––––––––––––––

In Memory of Mary Jane
and Curtis

PREFACE

This book reflects my best effort to make available to non-lawyers basic information that can help them craft individualized solutions to planning for the possibility (or reality) of disability. Informed by friendships dating to my childhood and enriched by professional study, I have long been interested in a variety of legal problems disabled people face. As someone who teaches about wills and trusts, I see a compelling need to plan for disability. It is a part of life virtually all of us will face, in one form or another, for some length of time. My hope is that this book will put you in a better position to work out a plan that suits you and those you love.

I owe debts of gratitude to the many who helped make this book possible. The University of Toledo College of Law provided financial support through my appointment as Charles W. Fornoff Professor of Law and Values. Friends too numerous to mention read and commented upon early drafts. Three different secretaries – Rae Eakin, Peggye Cummings, and Jennifer Drane – worked on the manuscript at various stages. Most importantly, my wife, Kyanne, has regularly supported me with her expertise and encouragement. I sincerely thank them all.

TABLE OF CONTENTS

Section IV. Teamwork

Section I

Getting Started

Chapter 1

Do I Need to Do This?

You've opened this book because someone recommended it or the title caught your eye, but you wonder, "Is this something that should concern me?" Consider a couple of potential stories.

Margaret, a widow since her 20s, built a career for herself in sales. She lived frugally and retired early. At 60, she moved to an apartment complex in the Southwest, and reveled in her independence. Unfortunately, six years later Margaret suffered a series of strokes which left her disoriented and unable to handle her own affairs. Margaret's niece, Helen, came to help and faced a mess: real estate in Illinois, a series of Certificates of Deposit held jointly with different nieces and nephews, and various bank and brokerage accounts in Margaret's own name. The only way for Helen to handle Margaret's finances was to get a court to declare Margaret incompetent and create a guardianship. By not anticipating the possibility that she might become disabled, Margaret created expenses for herself and frustrations for her favorite niece.

3

In contrast, Ruth and Chuck saw disability every day and thought about the future. In particular, they worried about their sons who had cerebral palsy. One was more independent, lived in a sheltered housing complex and could handle his own funds, but needed financial help. The other lived at home. What would happen to the boys when Ruth and Chuck no longer could help?

Seeking ideas, Ruth and Chuck located a lawyer who had worked with similarly-situated parents. Then the problems started. After a brief conference, the lawyer sent a draft will for Ruth and Chuck to review. The will was long and complex. Try as they might, Ruth and Chuck could make very little sense of it. They needed a clear source of information, so they could ask their lawyer the right questions and understand the answers.

This book is for people like Margaret, who should have thought ahead. And for Margaret's niece, who might have sent it to her aunt as a gift. And for Ruth and Chuck, to help bridge the gap with their lawyer (or help pick a better one). And for you, if you have a disabled child or parent or partner, or if you are concerned about what the future may hold for you.

The law provides a wide variety of opportunities for people who plan ahead. To take full advantage of those opportunities, however, you need to be well-informed. You needn't know the details of legal doctrine, but you should understand enough about the choices so that whatever plan develops is the cooperative effort of you and your advisors.

By now you may be asking, "What advisors? Can't I do this on my own?" The answer, of

Standardized forms aren't designed for *you*

course, is "Yes." But the next question becomes "At what cost?" You might buy a blank form at a business supply office or borrow a do-it-yourself book from the library. With either option, you could produce a low-cost, legally-binding document. A document designed to fit most people. Not a document designed to fit *you*.

Rather than forcing you to accept a "cookie cutter" plan just like someone else's, the law allows you to tailor a plan to your individual situation. Standardized forms, whether from a book or from a lazy lawyer, miss the opportunity to individualize a plan. Especially in the context of disability planning, standard plans fall far short of what you can accomplish with a little effort. When you know the basics, when you have thought about which options are best for you, you will be better able to work with your advisors to design a plan reflecting *your* needs and desires.

As an informed member of your planning team, you can be involved in the process, rather than just the recipient of other peoples' ideas of what's best for you. A team approach can be especially valuable because it draws together a variety of perspectives to assess your situation. Almost certainly, a lawyer should be on your team. Depending upon your needs, you may also want an insurance agent (or several), an accountant, or various other professionals. (We'll discuss teams in Section IV.) Whatever your situation, this book can help you become an active participant in the planning process.

Your participation is key because you can come up with your own approaches. One of the great things about this area of the law is that your options are not limited to the ideas noted here or those suggested by your advisors. There are a few limits, but on the whole, if you ask "Could I...?" the answer will be "Yes." By explaining key concepts and suggesting creative options, this book seeks to prompt you to come up with ideas to fit your family situation. You might want to keep a notepad nearby as you read along. Then you can jot down ideas and questions as they come to mind. Your notes can serve as the basis for putting in place a plan that is uniquely yours.

> **Jot down ideas.**

This book is structured to allow you to read through it from start to finish and to use it as a reference later. The following chapter introduces some basic concepts which provide background for the details to come later. The next section addresses ways to plan for financial security. Then we turn to issues surrounding health care decision-making. To help you implement your own plan, the book's final section provides suggestions for choosing and working with a team of advisors. For now, concentrate on the basic building blocks.

Chapter 2

Building Blocks

One way to understand the planning process is to visualize a child's collection of plastic blocks: bricks in many shapes and sizes, even some decorative pieces. Just as kids choose which bricks to use and how to arrange them, so do planners select among a wide array of legal devices to construct lifetime and estate plans to fit individual needs.

This chapter introduces basic terms and concepts—the bricks. Some topics may be familiar. Some may be new. The first several sections deal with property questions. Then we turn to various ways of empowering persons who can act on behalf of those who cannot decide for themselves. The chapter closes with an introduction to health care decision making. After reviewing this material, you will be in a better position to decide which of these subjects warrant your closer examination.

Probate

The term "probate" refers to systems with three basic functions: (1) collecting the assets owned by persons who have died, (2) resolving disputes among people—including creditors—who claim those assets, and (3) distributing what is left to the appropriate persons or institutions.

A common source of confusion is that only some property is "subject to probate." The chart below lists several forms of wealth that do not pass through the system. Notice the common characteristic of "non-probate" property: ownership is not solely in the hands of the person who died (the decedent).

Probate Property	Property Escaping Probate
o Property in your name only	o Life insurance benefits
o (usually) Your share of any community property	o Joint tenancies o Retirement benefits o Living trusts

Depending upon your situation, you may or may not have much probate property. For example, couples commonly hold some property as "joint tenants"—houses, cars, bank accounts, investments. When one partner dies, the survivor owns the property outright, because there is no one with whom to share it. That change happens automatically. There is no need to use the probate system to shift ownership of joint tenancies. Unless something changes before the *surviving* partner dies, however, we would need to use the probate system to handle that partner's assets.

If you are married and live in a state with community property, usually your half of the community property will pass through probate. In some states, your surviving spouse can get your share of the community property without probate (rather like the way joint tenancy works).

In recent years "avoiding probate" has been a hot topic. In many states, probate can be costly and time consuming. On the other hand, the fact that courts supervise the system means that probate offers protections against fraud, and in some places the costs are not very high.

Because you can avoid the probate system by placing wealth in the form of non-probate property, you should talk with your lawyer about whether probate avoidance should be one of your goals. Be sure to discuss the advantages and disadvantages of various alternatives to probate. In one sad case, a father decided to avoid probate by placing land in joint tenancy with his son. Later, the father remarried and wanted to undo the joint tenancy. When the son refused, the father sued him, but lost. The court said that the father had given the son a half interest in the land and couldn't get it back. By not appreciating that the joint tenancy could not be revoked—or by not anticipating the possibility of wanting to remarry—the father ended up alienating his son and spending a lot of money on lawyer's fees.

A side point about probate: probate avoidance is **NOT** tax avoidance. One of the most common mistakes people make is to think, "All my property is joint, so I'm avoiding estate tax." Rather, without much regard to the form in which property is held, the federal estate tax system taxes the wealth you *control.* (We'll talk more about estate taxes later in this chapter.)

In the next section we discuss what happens to the property that is subject to the probate system.

Intestacy and Wills

The law has established two basic systems to determine what to do with probate property after you die. If you don't have a valid will, a state law—called an intestate (in-tes´-tate) statute—will identify who gets your property. If you do have a will, it will cover the problem.

Technically, your "heirs" are those people whom the intestate statute identifies as taking your property. The details of these statutes vary from place to place, but they follow a common pattern. Your surviving spouse usually would share with your children, but may get the whole estate. If a child has died, the child's descendants (your grandchildren or great-grandchildren) will inherit your property. If neither your spouse nor any descendants survive, the property would go to your parents or their descendants (your brothers, sisters, nieces and nephews). If none of them survive, the statute designates more distant relatives to take the property. As a last resort, the state gets the property.

> **An intestate statute identifies your heirs.**

If you don't like the scheme of your state's intestate statute, you can create a will, which tells how to divide your probate property. (There are other reasons for making a will, like identifying someone to handle your estate or to be your children's guardian.)

> **A will says how you want your probate property divided.**

Almost always—especially if you plan to take care of a disabled person—you should consult a lawyer rather than relying on purchased forms or your own words.

Be especially careful if you select a plan that could leave one of your heirs unhappy (usually because someone gets a smaller share than if you had died intestate). The disappointed heir could challenge your will on the theory that you lacked capacity or were acting under someone's undue influence. Your lawyer can suggest a variety of ways of protecting your plan against such attacks.

For many people, especially those planning to handle a disability, a will does not offer enough flexibility. They need a trust, which we introduce in the next section and discuss in detail in Chapter 4.

Trusts

Trusts are the most useful single estate planning device. Simply put, a trust is an ownership arrangement in which someone (the trustee) holds and manages property to benefit someone else (the beneficiary). Depending upon local custom, the person creating the trust might be called a grantor, a trustor, a donor, or a settlor. This book will use the term "settlor." There can be more than one trustee, and several beneficiaries.

You can create a trust either during your lifetime or at death. A trust created during your lifetime is called a "living"

> **Trusts can be "living" or "testamentary"**

(or "inter vivos") trust. It can be used to manage your property for you or others. You keep the power to revoke the can also trust at any time. (Another alternative is to create, usually for tax reasons, a living trust that you cannot revoke.) A trust created by will is called a "testamentary" trust. Because the trust is part of your will, it gets no funds until your death and you can revoke it at any time.

Revocable living trusts have become very popular because they can be used for lots of purposes and at the same time their assets stay out of the probate system. For example, you could put your property in a trust and name yourself as trustee with the duty to pay yourself the trust income during your life-time and to spend trust assets in your behalf (say, for emergencies). At your death a new trustee could distribute the remaining assets among the people you identify.

One problem that arises under such a plan is people often forget that they are acting as "trustee," rather than as individuals. For example, suppose you sell some property you've already put into the trust. If you use the cash to buy a replacement investment, you might neglect to put the replacement into the trust. Even if you are confident about using the trust to avoid probate, it's always a good idea to have a will as a backup to cover whatever items the trust may have missed. Otherwise, that property will be distributed according to the intestate statute.

Austin W. Scott, a famous Harvard professor, once commented that "[t]he purposes for which trusts can be created are as unlimited as the imagination of lawyers." He should have added "and their clients." This book seeks to stimulate your thinking so that you and your advisors can create a plan to fit your individual needs. Often, a trust will be the centerpiece of the plan you develop.

Another way to pass wealth to survivors is to purchase life insurance, our next topic.

Life Insurance

The life insurance industry in recent years has offered a wide variety of new products. Nonetheless, two basic features appear. Some policies are pure term insurance covering the risk of someone dying during the term of the policy. Other policies include the term protection, but add some form of an investment feature as well. Because the features vary widely, you should examine the options carefully and consult with your planning team about which best suit your needs.

Rather than having insurance proceeds paid directly to individual beneficiaries, many people name a trustee as the policy's beneficiary, so the death benefit is added to other trust property. This technique is a particularly popular way to provide financial support for a disabled person. Unless the insurance proceeds are paid to the estate of someone or to a testamentary trust, those death benefits avoid probate.

A knowledgeable insurance agent can be an important member of your planning team. We often

> **A good insurance agent can help.**

undervalue insurance agents because we view them merely as sellers of products and some are only that. Many agents, however, are very well-informed professionals who can educate other members of the team about different planning options.

16

Taking the time to get to know a good insurance agent can be a great investment in your and your family's future.

Distribution Schemes

Whether you use a will, a trust, life insurance or all three, ultimately you may want to divide all or part of your property among different beneficiaries. If you have a disabled child, for example, you may want to provide separately for that child while treating your other children as a group. Over time, several common patterns have emerged for dividing property among a group of family members. As usual, you can modify or combine these ideas to meet your needs. Don't let a lawyer's form push you into a division you don't want.

Sometimes these different approaches yield the same division, especially if the survivors are all in one or two generations. On the other hand, if survivors are spread out among several generations, different approaches can yield drastically different distributions. You can create these distribution patterns for descendants (children, grandchildren) and for other relatives.

To see the choices, consider the family tree below. (Brackets indicate people who have died. Survivors are in **bold**.) George has died, a widower whose three children all died before he did. Alice left one child (Katie) and two grandchildren

(Jack's children, Ursa and Victor). Bob's daughter Lisa also died before George, but Lisa's son Warren survived. Carol had three children, only one of whom (Olaf) survived George. Carol's daughter Mary left Xavier, and Carol's son Nate left Yenta and Zoe.

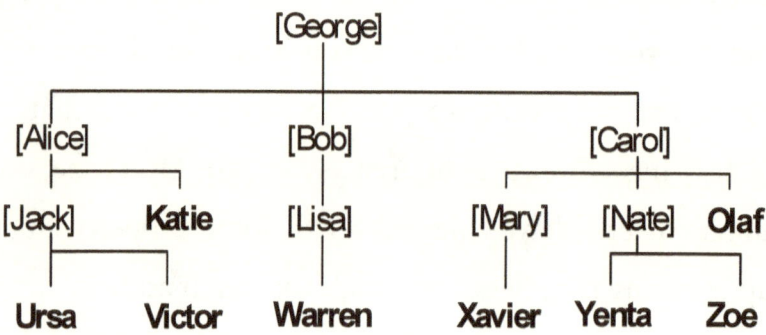

Per Capita. One possibility would be to divide George's estate or trust on a "per capita" basis. This system just counts heads, without regard to which generation a beneficiary belongs. Each of George's eight surviving descendants would take a 1/8 share, as shown in the diagram on the next page.

Per Capita

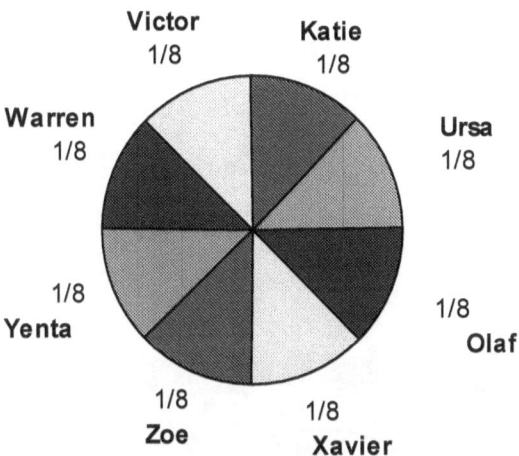

Per Stirpes. Many documents still use this old term, which means "by the stocks." Some documents instead say "by right of representation." The problem with both terms is that courts don't agree on what they mean. The most common interpretation is "divide my estate into as many shares as I had children who either survived me or left descendants who survived me." If that is the scheme you want, it is better to say so, rather than rely on words like "per stirpes" or "by right of representation."

Under this interpretation, the law views a family in vertical terms: Alice's family, Bob's family, and Carol's family. Thus, we initially would divide George's estate into three shares, and then subdivide from there. Half of Alice's 1/3 would go to Katie

(1/6), and the other half would be divided between Ursa and Victor (1/12 each). Warren would get all of Bob's third. Carol's third initially would be split three ways, with Olaf taking one of those (1/9 of the whole). Xavier gets Mary's share (1/9), while Yenta and Zoe divide Nate's (for 1/18 each). The division would look like this:

Per Stirpes

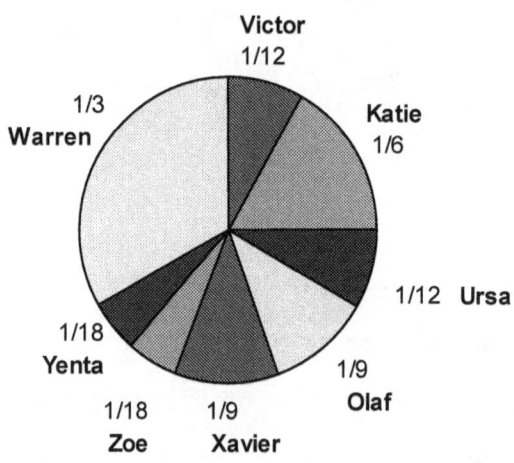

The other way courts have interpreted "per stirpes" is to divide the estate at the oldest generation containing survivors. In our example, this interpretation would have us skip George's children's generation because all of them died before George. Instead, we divide the estate at the grandchildren's level, and again subdivide from there. Now we have six shares, with Katie and Olaf each getting 1/6. Warren and Xavier each get their re-spective mother's share (1/6). Ursa and Victor divide Jack's share (1/12 each), as Yenta and Zoe similarly divide Nate's share (1/12 each). That division would look like this:

Per Capita With Representation

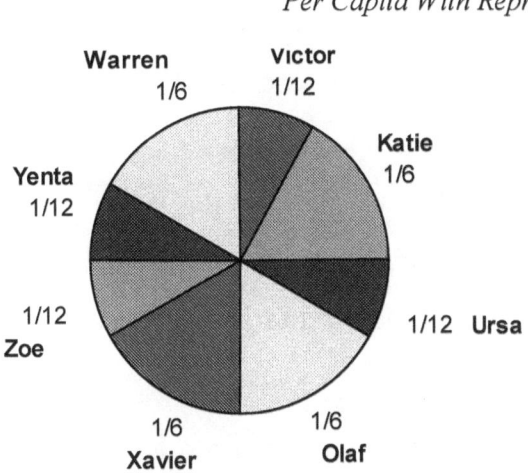

To help clear up the confusion some courts have started calling the first interpretation "strict per stirpes" and the second approach "per capita with representation." Rather than using terms like these, however, your documents should identify clearly the appropriate generation for dividing the estate.

Per Capita at Each Generation. Recently, a different way of dividing estates has gained popularity. Rather than looking at each family in vertical terms, "per capita at each generation"

21

views families horizontally, treating each generation equally. The division starts at the oldest generation that leaves survivors. Rather than subdividing from that level, however, this approach puts all that's left into a pot and shares it equally among the next generation. In our example, we'd again start at the grand-children's level and give Katie and Olaf 1/6 each. Then we take the rest (2/3 of the whole) and divide it equally among Ursa, Victor, Warren, Xavier, Yenta and Zoe (1/9 each). Under this approach, the great-grandchildren get equal shares, rather than having the size of their gifts determined by how many children their parents and grandparents had. The division would look like this:

Per Capita at Each Generation

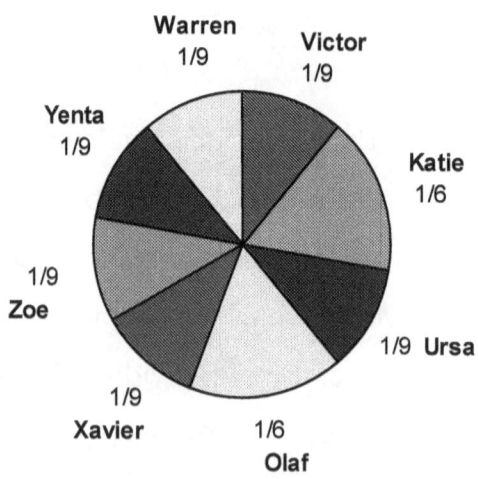

There is no right or wrong way to divide your estate. The choices are endless. As you select one, keep in mind that "fair" may not mean "equal." But beware of creating family unhappiness, which can last a long time. The important point is to consider several alternatives, choose one you like, and be sure your documents express in detail how to accomplish the division.

However you divide it, if you have enough of it, you'll need to consider the impact of estate taxes, to which we now turn.

Estate Tax

A comprehensive discussion of tax planning is beyond the scope of this book. The following sketch, however, should help you to determine if you need to get more information.

The first step is to tally up your wealth. Recall that probate-avoidance is **NOT** estate tax-avoidance. As a rule of thumb, if you can get your hands on property now or can control where it goes after your death, the property will be in your federal "gross estate." Thus, the overwhelming bulk of non-probate property - including life insurance proceeds, your share of joint property, retirement benefits, and property in revocable trusts - is subject to estate tax. If your total wealth (including that of your spouse) is approaching $1,500,000, you

> **Tally up all of your wealth.**

need to consider some tax planning. (Recent changes in the tax code provide that the magic number will increase in steps so that by 2009 it will be $3.5 million and then the tax may expire, unless Congress changes course.) The code gives each of us a tax credit, which effectively shelters estates up to that amount. If your wealth—again, broadly defined—is likely to stay less than that and you have not made substantial lifetime gifts, you need not worry about federal estate tax.

If tax planning is appropriate and you are married, you should consider planning options that will allow both you and your spouse to use your tax credits. A properly structured plan can pass double the individual exemption amount, tax free. Do not delay, however. The benefit of using both tax credits is usually lost unless the plan has been completed before one spouse dies.

Powers of Attorney

Here we introduce the power of attorney, a topic we'll cover in more detail in Chapter 3. A power of attorney is a document one person (the principal) uses to authorize another (the agent) to act for the principal while the principal is alive. The principal must be competent when the agent is named, but—as we shall see—the agent may also be able to act for a disabled principal. By the way, despite the term "attorney," the agent need not be a lawyer.

In the context of planning for incapacity, the term "power of attorney" can be source of confusion. Traditionally,

> **A "Power of Attorney" may cover many areas.**

such powers enabled one person to handle the property of another. More recently, legislatures have authorized people to name others to make health care decisions on their behalf. The confusion comes because both types of documents may carry the title "Power of Attorney." To help avoid the problem, some planners have started to reserve the "Power of Attorney" title for property matters and to use "Health Care Proxy" to label the document granting authority to make health care decisions. This book will follow that trend, and this section will introduce the property power.

Sometimes people will execute a power of attorney for a very specific purpose or a specific time period. For example, if you had to be out of town at the time set for closing the sale of a house, you might authorize someone else to sign the papers for you. More commonly, powers of attorney authorize the agent to act in a wide variety of situations.

At one time, the agent's power ended if the principal became incapacitated. Because planners saw the potential for using powers in just that situation, they convinced legislatures to authorize "durable" powers, which continue to be good despite

Durable powers survive incapacity.

the principal's inca-
pacity. Even durable
powers, however, are not valid after the principal's death.

Guardianships

When someone is a minor or is unable to make various kinds of decisions and no one has the power to decide, the law provides for a guardian to make decisions on that person's behalf. Sometimes courts appoint guardians named in a will to care for minor children. If there was no will, a court will decide with the help of family members, friends, or social workers. In other situations, a court can appoint a guardian for an incompetent adult.

By the way, your state may not use the term "guardian." For our purposes, "guardian" includes "conservator," "curator," "committee" and like terms identifying the person or people making decisions for others. Fortunately, most places at least agree on the single term "wards" when referring to the people who cannot act for themselves.

In general, in order for a court to appoint a guardian, the ward must be "incompetent," by being either too young or unable to handle their affairs. Not so long ago, guardianship was an all-or-nothing proposition almost everywhere. A ward lost virtually all decision-making authority. Increasingly, states have recognized that someone might be incompetent to make some decisions, but able to make others.

Many states have reformed their laws to allow "limited" or "partial" guardianships, so that a guardian for an adult might be named for some purposes but not others. Typically, the basic standard is whether the ward can understand the question at hand, what the options are, and what the likely consequences of a particular decision will be. If the ward cannot, a guardian can be appointed to handle that particular decision (or category of decisions). Thus, someone might be incompetent for one purpose, but competent for another. For example, they may be able to handle small amounts of money, but unable to manage investments. Because of these different approaches, it is very important to learn about your state's laws on guardianship before deciding whether to pursue this option.

Beware of being over-protective. As we question whether a particular adult friend or relative needs a guardian, we also must guard against our own over-protectiveness or even selfishness. Decisions with which we disagree are not necessarily irrational. Families have created a great deal of pain for themselves by calling on the guardianship system when it was not appropriate to do so.

In the planning context, the law distinguishes between

There are two basic kinds of guardians.

two different types of guardian-ships. A *guardian of the person* has the responsibility to care for the personal needs of the ward. Guardians of the person handle topics like setting bedtimes and monitoring TV viewing for a minor or supervising travel plans or personal hygiene for an adult. A court may also appoint the same person or another (even an institution) as *guardian of the property* of the ward. This person would handle some or all of the ward's financial affairs.

If you anticipate the need for one or more guardians for a disabled person in your care, you can use your will to identify people you believe a court should appoint. In most situations, it is best to name someone younger than yourself and to indicate a possible successor guardian in case your first choice cannot serve.

Take special care in selecting guardians, for they will

Choose a guardian carefully.

have real power over their wards. Consider the nature of your relative's disability. Would the guardian need to super-vise medication or make other health care decisions? Provide counseling? Arrange for housing? Consider both personalities. How would the guardian and ward get along? What are the chances that the guardian could be abusive? On the financial side, consider the guardian's honesty and ability. Would the guardian seek to profit from the arrangement? Is the guardian conscientious? No matter whom you select, be sure to meet with the potential guardian and discuss—fully—the ward's needs. Do your best to avoid surprises. (See Chapter 9 for suggestions on how to do that.)

Courts supervise guardians. Such oversight can help avoid arbitrary, or even fraudulent, activity. Especially if your family is divided on what to do, a guardian backed by the prestige and power of a court may be the best solution. Be cautioned, however, that while some courts provide excellent oversight, other courts are so busy that as a practical matter they rubber-stamp guardians' actions without careful review. One factor in deciding whether to use the guardianship option should be the level of review courts conduct where the ward lives.

Guardianship also presents significant disadvantages. For one thing, because it labels the ward as at least partially "incompetent," it carries a stigma and a cost to the ward's self-esteem. In states where guardianship is an all-or-nothing proposition, a court finding of incompetence can have profound effects on the ward by denying the power to make even the simplest decisions.

| **Guardianships have disadvantages.** |

Because it is court-supervised, guardianship is also costly, in terms of both time and money. Quick decisions may be hard to get. Evaluations, hearings, reports and the like all take time and drive up costs. In short, the protections of court supervision are not free.

In many states, guardians of property work under restrictions that limit flexibility. The list of allowable investments may be short, eliminating the possibility of buying mutual fund shares or common stocks. The law may inhibit (or even prohibit) some kinds of spending, like making gifts to others or taking a vacation.

For a variety of reasons, many people decide to leave guardianship as a last resort. At least where adults are concerned, creative use of caretakers (on the personal side) and of trusts or powers of attorney (on the property management side) often can avoid the need for guardianship. In the next section, we shift our emphasis from mostly financial questions to very personal ones about health care.

Health Care Decisions

Competent adults can resolve their own health care choices. Incompetent individuals, however, need someone else to make those decisions. For people who have never been competent, like severely retarded adults, guardians probably will have that power.

People who are competent, but anticipate the possibility of not being able to decide in the future, have two basic options which we introduce here and cover in detail in Part III. Both

> **Living wills and health care proxies are different.**

options fall under the label "advance directive." One is executing a "living will," which gives instructions to health care providers on how to proceed in specified situations. Another option is a "health care proxy" (also known as a Durable Power of Attorney for Health Care Decisions). The proxy names someone else to make decisions on behalf of the disabled person. Some people execute both documents; some states allow one document to include both features.

To protect the people who have not executed an advance directive and have no guardian, many states appoint "surrogate decision makers" according to a list set by statute. If you are in a non-traditional relationship and want your partner to have decision making authority, it is especially important to execute an advance directive. Most statutes put non-relatives far down (or off) the list of favored surrogates.

A common sentiment is "I don't want to lie there, kept alive by machines." Most of us, however, would not want that rule applied in all situations. If we have a heart attack, catch pneumonia, or suffer a serious accident, we'd like to be on a respirator until we can recover. The problem we face is trying to decide ahead of time which situations call for using the machines and which call for turning them off. Before you sign a living will, think carefully about what it says. Before you name someone to decide in your behalf under a health care proxy, talk over your views with the person you appoint.

Our final section clears up some of the confusion about government health care support systems.

Medicare and Medicaid

Because of their similar names, these two government programs are often confused. Medicare is the federal health insurance program for elderly and disabled persons. Medicaid is the joint federal–state welfare program to pay specified health care costs for persons of limited means. Because of the heavy state involvement in Medicaid, benefits may vary widely between states. Each of these programs has developed its own complex bureaucracies and volumes of detailed regulations. Because adequate descriptions of these programs provisions can occupy entire books, no effort will be made here to attempt a summary. If you do consult materials on Medicare or Medicaid, be sure to get the latest information. The rules change fre-quently, and much printed material is out of date.

Now that you have the basic building blocks in mind, let's look at some of the ways to design a plan that fits your needs.

Questions to Consider

➢ Do I need a will?

➢ Should I consider a trust?

➢ Do I need life insurance?

➢ How would I like my property divided?

➢ Do I need to do estate tax planning?

➢ Should I consider a durable power of attorney?

➢ Should I consider naming a guardian?

➢ Should I consider a living will or
health care proxy?

Section II

Financial Security Planning

Financial Security Planning

In the last chapter, we learned about the high personal and financial costs of guardianship. Now we turn to questions like "What are the alternatives?" and "How can they best be structured to facilitate my goals?"

We start with a closer look at the most common and least expensive way to handle property of a disabled person: powers of attorney. Then we turn to trusts, which offer more flexibility and precision. Next, this section examines questions about how to coordinate private support with governmental benefit programs. Finally, we introduce long-term care insurance. As always, the goal is to help you get your creative juices flowing, so you and your planning team can develop the best possible approaches for your situation.

Chapter 3

Durable Power of Attorney

You'll recall from Chapter 2 that a power of attorney authorizes one person (the agent) to act on behalf of another (the principal) while the principal is alive. By executing a durable power while you are competent, you can name someone to handle your financial affairs should you become incapacitated. Durable powers are popular because they can serve as relatively inexpensive "insurance" against incapacity.

Why You Need a Durable Power of Attorney

You may be asking, "Do I really need a durable power of attorney?" Try asking yourself some more questions.

- Do you get checks made out to you? If you became incapacitated, no one could cash them without creating a guardianship.

- Do you own assets—including property owned with someone else—that would require your signature to sell? If you became incapacitated, no one could sell them without creating a guardianship.

Remember also that incapacity need not be permanent; a serious accident could knock you off your feet for several months. Most of us would benefit from having created a durable power of attorney.

Choosing an Agent

When considering a power of attorney, you should first identify people who might serve as your agent. Think of several people and compare their qualities and talents. Most of all, you'll want someone you can trust. Be skeptical here. Some otherwise honest people become sorely tempted when they have access to someone else's money. Be wary of creating conflicts of interest by naming someone who might

> **When choosing an agent, be skeptical.**

benefit from being stingy with you. For example, naming a son or daughter may seem like the best idea until you consider that they may be reluctant to spend money on your behalf, so more will be left for them. If you have several children, naming one may create jealousy and conflict; perhaps you should name all of them, to act only on a majority vote. (If you think you can't trust anyone, jump to Chapter 9.)

Your agent also should be able to make financial decisions. The nature and extent of your assets will go a long way in determining how much expertise your agent will need. Remember that even if you don't have vast resources, your agent should be someone who can handle the insurance or government claim forms that accompany almost any incapacity.

Most commonly, agents are family members or trusted friends who are willing to help out. Sometimes lawyers or other professionals act under a power of attorney. They usually charge a fee for the service. Before granting such powers to someone you don't know very well, make a special effort to investigate that person's honesty and reliability.

Also, consider the possibility that your agent might die or otherwise be unable to serve. Your document should name a successor agent to take over if your first choice can't serve. In most situations, your choice for successor agent should be someone younger than yourself.

Overcoming Common Problems

Durable powers also carry risks. By knowing the risks, you can better avoid them. The biggest problem is that third

> **The biggest problem is that third parties may not honor the power.**

parties—banks, insurance companies, stock brokers—may not honor the power. Concerned that a person claiming to be an agent may not really have the authority to act, those third parties may simply refuse to cooperate. Here are the main objections third parties raise when they decide whether to honor a durable power.

Objection 1: Did the principal have the mental capacity to create the power?

This can become a real problem for people who don't anticipate the possibility of disability. Once someone can no longer handle their own affairs, it is usually too late to execute a power of attorney (or, for that matter, a will or a trust). There are two lessons here: (1) execute documents before there is any question about capacity and (2) create a record so that you can prove capacity if it is questioned later.

Many people who face declining capacity find they have "good days" and "bad days." If they execute legal documents on one of the good days when they understand what's going on, the documents will be valid. The problem is proving that, in fact, it was done on a good day.

Solution: Good Witnesses. Although most states do not require wit-

| Create a record. |

nesses for a power of attorney to be valid, good witnesses can help overcome later doubts about whether the principal had the mental capacity to execute the document. To insulate your power of attorney against such concerns, you might ask witnesses to sign—before a notary public—a statement that they had discussed with you what powers the agent would be getting and how the power of attorney would work. The statement should also say that the witnesses believed you understood the document and its implications. A statement for witnesses might look like this one: "On March 17, 2003, we met with Donna Pruselli and discussed the Power of Attorney she gave to Dorothy Pizzimenti. Donna understood that Dorothy will have the power to act in Donna's behalf in a wide range of financial affairs, including the powers to sign checks, sell assets and make gifts." Attaching such a statement to the power of attorney should help convince third parties to honor the document.

Objection 2: Is the principal "incapacitated"?

Many states allow a "springing" power of attorney, which is not effective until an event usually disability of the principal takes place. In other words, there is no power until it is needed. Sometimes disputes arise about whether the principal really is disabled, thus kicking in the power. To avoid this problem, a power should define "disabled" and probably should identify a group of people (with flexible membership) to decide whether the principal meets the definition.

This question arises if the power is a "springing" power that is not effective until the principal becomes incapacitated. Suppose you have been named agent under a springing power your Uncle Juan executed, and he now needs your help. Before honoring your power, someone will want to know if it has "sprung." For example, if your agent wants to cash in a Certificate of Deposit for you, the bank will want some assurance that you now lack capacity and therefore has authority to act in your behalf.

Solution One: Use a presently-effective power. One way to avoid the problem is not to use a springing power at all. If you create a power which becomes effective immediately (and which continues to be effective after any incapacity), the problem about capacity never would come up. To maintain control while competent, you can ask your agent not to use the power unless incapacity arises.

Of course, by creating a presently-effective power you would be giving someone authority before you really needed help. In some situations, family harmony might better be preserved if no one had any power until the last possible moment. Then a springing power might work best.

Some people like the idea of a springing power because they don't trust their agent to wait until the principal becomes incompetent. That's not a good reason to use a springing power. If you don't trust the person who would be your agent, choose another agent.

Solution Two: Define "incapacitated" and identify a team to decide. If you want a springing power, it's best to use two steps. First, define the circumstances under which the power will spring into action, usually when you become "incapacitated." Second, identify three people you trust, and let any two of them decide whether the incapacity has occurred.

For example, the document might read:

> "For purposes of this document the principal is 'incapacitated' if in the opinion of two members of the certifying team the principal is unable to make informed decisions regarding his [or her]

financial affairs. The certifying team shall consist of Dr. Jane McDonald [primary care physician], John Robertson [trusted friend], and Robin Kennelty [accountant, lawyer or other advisor]. If any members of the certifying team cannot serve, the remaining member(s) shall appoint replacement members."

Your team should be people you trust to make a fair evaluation should the need arise. To enhance credibility, at least one team member should be a physician. To avoid conflicts, the team should <u>not</u> include the person you are naming as agent nor anyone closely connected to the agent.

If it becomes necessary to use the power, two members of the team could sign a statement certifying the incapacity. Attaching that statement to the power should relieve any third party's concerns about whether the power had indeed sprung into action.

Objection 3: Does the power authorize this activity?

Uncertainty about the scope of the agent's authority is probably the most common problem that powers of attorney present. Even very broad language giving the agent "authority to do all other acts on my behalf" may not be enough to allow the agent to do specific things, like selling a house or making gifts.

Solution: Think broadly and be specific. Taking time to consider your potential needs is particularly important. First, make a list of the financial tasks you do over a two or three month period:

- cash checks from your employer, investments, the government, or insurance
- purchase food, clothes, household supplies
- pay bills
- buy or sell stocks and mutual funds
- sign proxy statements
- renew certificates of deposit...

Next, list things you do less frequently:

- file tax returns
- pay a child's or grandchild's tuition
- buy a car or a house
- sign a lease...

The list you develop should fit your personal situation. As you compile your list, consider whether you'd want your agent to be able to do the following things:

Make gifts. Gift situations arise in two contexts. First are the charitable, holiday, birthday, and special occasion gifts most people regularly give. Second are gifts made as part of a plan to reduce income or estate taxes. Because in the narrow economic sense, gift-giving means taking property away from the principal, courts are very reluctant to allow gifts unless the power specifically authorizes them.

> **Set guidelines for gift giving.**

Details are especially important. What charities? Perhaps include a non-exclusive list of favorites. Whose birthdays? Perhaps say "children, grandchildren, and their spouses" and then list any special others. How often and how much? Give guidelines or set maximums.

Sell important assets. Suppose you will not be able to return home. Can your agent sell it? Even though the document may grant authority "to sell any of my assets," potential buyers may be reluctant to recognize the power if the sale involves a major asset, like a house or business property. Again, the more specific the document is, the more likely it will be honored. (On the other hand, there is a danger in being *too* specific. Authority to sell "my 1998 Jeep Cherokee" would not likely extend to another vehicle.)

Run a business. You may want someone to be able to step in and take over your business, especially for the short term. As with your personal life, consider the things you do in a business capacity: hire and fire employees, issue paychecks, order inventory.

Pay taxes. Some taxing authorities want very specific authorization, so be sure to include authority to file forms with, settle disputes with, and pay taxes to "any local, state, or federal taxing authorities."

Change legal residency. For any number of reasons—tax advantages, convenience of other family members. Medicaid qualification—it may make sense to change the state of your legal residency. Consider giving your agent the authority to move you to a different state.

Create or fund a trust. If after reading the next chapter you think a trust might become useful someday, but you don't want to create one yet, you might consider authorizing your agent to

> **An agent's power to create a trust can be very useful if the principal's incapacity lasts a long time.**

create one for you. You might even have the trust document prepared ahead of time so you know all the details, and then

give your agent the power "to execute the trust document dated
_____ and located in my safe deposit box." If you already
have a trust, consider giving your agent authority to add funds
to the trust and to revoke or amend it.

Qualify for government benefits As we'll see in Chapter 5, some government programs—like Medicaid—allow you
to keep assets in some forms (but not others) and still qualify
for benefits. You may want to give your agent the authority to
convert your resources into forms that won't endanger your eligibility for government aid.

Once you have created a good list of powers, take it to

Watch for powers you don't want to grant.

your lawyer and
ask for suggestions
of things you might add. But be careful. Although the lawyer's
list may include many ideas worth considering, look carefully
for powers you don't want to grant. (Once, when we had to be
out of town on the date scheduled for closing our house purchase, my wife and I needed a power of attorney to allow someone to sign the papers. Our lawyer offered us a form that in-
cluded the power to commit us to a mental institution!) Finally,
if you want to make especially clear that the agent not have a
specific power, say so.

Objection 4: Has the principal revoked the power?

You can revoke your power of attorney at any time while you remain competent. Thus, third parties may be concerned that a power is not valid because it has been revoked. Because a power can always be revoked even the day it is executed, there is no complete solution to this problem.

Partial Solution One: Execute new documents periodically. Older powers run a greater risk of having been revoked, so third parties are more likely to honor powers executed recently. Periodically executing new documents increases the chance that your power will be more current if it is needed. Check with your lawyer to see what time period is likely to be acceptable to your financial institutions.

Partial Solution Two: Attach a "not revoked" statement. If the principal becomes incompetent, the "durable" feature of the power kicks in and the power is no longer revocable. Therefore, it can be helpful to attach to the power a statement from credible witnesses that the principal is no longer competent and, to their knowledge, the power has never been revoked. If a springing power is involved, you might include such a statement when the team certifies incapacity.

Partial Solution Three: Include a "hold harmless" provision. Some third parties will take comfort from a statement that they will not be held liable if they honor the document in good faith, believing that it had not been revoked.

Durable powers of attorney can be useful in a wide variety of situations and should be part of your planning. When thinking ahead—especially about disability—you shouldn't stop with durable powers. Trusts can provide a wider range of security and choices than can durable powers. The next chapter offers the opportunity to consider these valuable tools for disability planning.

Questions to Consider

➢ Who should serve as my agent?

➢ Do I want a springing power?

➢ What powers do I want to give my agent?

➢ What powers do I <u>not</u> want to give?

➢ Has my situation changed, so I need a new power?

Chapter 4

Trusts: Personalized Protection

Upon hearing the words "trust fund," many people will think of playboys sailing around the world and will conclude, "I'm not rich. Trusts aren't for me." But you don't have to be rich for a trust to make sense for you. Moreover, because trusts are flexible tools, you and your lawyer can shape one to fit your particular situation.

The best way to get personalized protection is to talk with your lawyer about *your* family's needs and *your* preferences for how to meet them. This chapter can help by raising questions and presenting options for you to consider. You may want to review Chapter 2's introduction to trusts.

First we will discuss the advantages trusts offer over other solutions discussed in earlier chapters. Then we will examine how to choose a trustee and whether to name a trust advisor. Next, we'll take a brief look at trustee fees. Then we turn to a discussion of whether and how to use an advocate for your disabled beneficiary. This chapter closes with ideas about special powers and duties to assign to your trustee and which of your assets you might want to place in trust.

51

Advantages of Trusts

"Why," you might ask, "should I go to the trouble and expense of setting up a trust?" Maybe you won't want a trust. Before you decide, however, you should *consider* whether a trust makes sense for you. Only then can you judge whether the benefits outweigh the costs.

Chapter 2 discussed the two primary ways to avoid probate: creating joint tenancies with other people or creating living trusts. Once you establish a joint tenancy, you cannot later change your mind and revoke it. In contrast, you can establish a trust and at the same time keep the power to revoke the trust if you want to.

Some disabled people create a joint tenancy bank account to allow another person to handle the disabled person's finances. Sometimes this arrangement works well, but sometimes disputes arise about how the money is spent or who owns the balance if the disabled person dies. A trust can minimize or avoid those problems.

Trusts also have advantages over powers of attorney. Banks, stockbrokers and others are likely to recognize the authority of a trustee, even if they would question someone acting under a power of attorney. In addition, the law of trusts has established answers to many questions, but the law surrounding powers of attorney is not as well-developed, so more problems might arise interpreting powers of attorney.

Trusts also offer another advantage: they can last longer than one person's lifetime. Trusts can protect your spouse and surviving children. In contrast, if you give a power of attorney to someone, that person will have no authority to act after your death.

Choosing Trustees

If you decide to create a trust, one of your most important decisions will be selecting a trustee. As we'll see, by carefully structuring your plan, you can do much to help your trustee accomplish your goals. All the creative planning in the world, however, won't make up for a bad trustee. Your trustee—either alone or working with others—must be able to handle two basic kinds of duties: (1) asset management and (2) personal decision making.

> **Your trustee should have both business and personal skills.**

Your trustee should be someone (or some institution, like a bank) who can manage investments and prepare reports and tax forms. The trustee should be able to select investments which fit the various beneficiaries' situations as they change over time. (For example, if the trust is likely to continue for a long time, riskier investments may make sense because they could generate higher returns and there would be time to recover from losses.) In addition, the trustee must keep track of checks and receipts, bills and financial reports. For some tasks, the trustee may have to consult experts, but frequent use of expert advisors can both bog down the process and drive up costs. The more the trustee can do—and do well—without help, the better.

On the personal side, your trustee must have a very different set of skills. You will want a trustee who appreciates each beneficiary's capabilities, goals, and needs. Your trustee should have both skill and interest in communicating. Your trustee should have good judgment and be fair.

Because finding a single person with all these talents can be difficult, some people combine professional competence and personal attention by appointing two co-trustees. One— usually a professional or a bank—handles the asset management, and the other—usually a family member or trusted friend—makes the personal decisions. This arrangement takes some of the paperwork burden off the family member or friend, and it adds a personal touch to what sometimes can be an impersonal business person or corporation.

Having a neutral professional involved also can reduce family tensions. Sometimes it can be hard for a relative or friend to say "No" to a beneficiary who makes an unreasonable request.

In addition, if the trustee is also a beneficiary, the trustee may have a conflict of interest: by saying "No" to a request from someone else, the trustee may be increasing his or her own share of the trust. An independent trustee would not face either problem.

On the other hand, co-trustee arrangements have some disadvantages. The law in most states requires the trustees to agree before either can act. This rule can prompt inaction if they can't agree. Even if agreement is likely, it takes time. Getting approval for each investment or each distribution can be un-wieldy. One solution to this problem is for the trust docu-ment to assign different duties to each trustee. For example, the professional trustee might have sole authority over investments. In some states, if the document gives one trustee sole authority over some areas, the excluded trustee is not liable for losses suffered as a result of those decisions. In other states, the law is unclear, so each trustee may be liable for the mistakes of the other. Attempts to divide duties among trustees can also lead to disputes about which trustee has responsibility for a particular decision.

> **You may want co-trustees or a trust advisor.**

One way to avoid the problems of co-trustees would be to name a single trustee, but then ask a trusted friend or relative to serve as a "trust advisor." Depending upon the personalities

involved, you might structure the relationship between the trustee and the advisor different ways:

- You could require the trustee to consult with
  the advisor before deciding whether and how
  to spend trust funds for a beneficiary. The
  ultimate authority would stay with the trustee.

- You could require the trustee to get the advisor's approval for any such decision. Of
  course, this approach would set up the possibility of a conflict.

- You could give the advisor the power to order the trustee to spend funds as the advisor
  directs.

By using a trust advisor, you can bring some flexibility to
the traditional trust where the trustee has all the power, while
at the same time avoiding the need for (and complications of) a
co-trustee arrangement.

If you decide to appoint a person as a trustee or if you
name a trust advisor, be sure to consider

Age is a factor.

that person's age, in addition to his or her
talents. How long do you expect the trust to last? How likely is

your choice to live that long? Notice that corporate trustees are more likely to be around for a long time.

Your trust should provide some method for choosing successor trustees (and, if applicable, new trust advisors). Despite your best efforts, the trustees you select may not work out. They may be unresponsive or incompetent. They may die prematurely. To deal with these possibilities, your trust might give trusted family members or friends the power to remove a trustee or add one or replace one who has resigned or died.

Trustee Fees

As you weigh the decision about whether to name a professional trustee, you may be tempted to avoid the fees a professional would charge. You may expect a family member or friend would work for free. Be careful, on several grounds.

First, expecting someone to go uncompensated may not be fair. Being a trustee means taking on a lot of responsibility and often spending a great deal of time on the task. Some compensation, even at a reduced rate, may be appropriate. Moreover, you don't want your trustee to treat the job casually. Even those with the best intentions may lose interest over time. Honorable people who are accepting fees may be more likely to remain attentive.

Second, before rejecting a professional's fee as too high,

> **Check fee arrangements carefully.**

find out what services it covers. For example, a bank's fee typically will include the cost of obtaining investment advice, preparing tax returns, and preparing regular reports to beneficiaries. In many situations, trust officers will be able to answer their own legal questions, thus saving the need for lawyer's fees. A non-professional trustee may need to hire investment advisors, accountants and lawyers. It might be cheaper to go with the professional trustee in the first place.

Third, beware of being "penny wise and pound foolish." It may be worth paying more for greater expertise.

As a practical matter, the size of your trust may determine whether you select a professional trustee. In some large cities, banks won't accept trusts smaller than $200,000. Even if they do, their fees for smaller trusts may be too high. In other places, $50,000 may be the lower limit. Some states allow smaller trusts to be "pooled" together to create larger, more economically-efficient units. We'll discuss pooled trusts in Chapter 5. In any case, before deciding whether to name a professional trustee, ask around about fees.

Using An Advocate

One advantage of planning for disability is that it gives you the chance to name someone to be an advocate for a disabled beneficiary. For example, an Alzheimer's patient may be confined to a nursing home, or a severely retarded young adult may be living in a mental institution. People in situations like these often benefit from having someone else watching out for their personal needs. Are the sheets being changed? When was the last outing? How is the new medication working out? Such concerns may be beyond the interest or expertise of a trustee, especially a professional one. One solution is to name an advocate. The advocate might be the same person who serves as the trust advisor, or it might be someone else.

Pause for a moment before you say, "What a good idea. I'd really like to know someone will take care of _____." Ask whether that person *really* needs to be "taken care of." By providing too much protec-

Would an advocate help or hurt?

tion, well-meaning people—especially parents of disabled children—can inhibit the growth of people they love. Often the best gift for a disabled person is independence. By appointing an advocate, you may be robbing your loved one of the satisfaction that comes from handling one's own problems.

Some people who cannot look out for themselves will live in residential facilities of various kinds. Some of these facilities are excellent, with well-trained, caring staffs. Unfortunately, that is not always the case. In many places care providers are poorly paid workers with minimal training and little experience. Professional staff may treat all residents the same, despite the need for individualized care. An advocate can greatly improve the quality of life of people needing such care.

Selecting the right advocate can be challenging. It should be someone who lives nearby and is carefully tuned to the beneficiary's needs and preferences, yet at the same time assertive enough to provide meaningful protection. It should be someone with common sense, a generous heart, and the ability to ask tough questions. You may want to ask different people to take responsibility for different aspects of the beneficiary's life. If you can, identify an alternative advocate, in case your first choice cannot continue to serve. In addition, the advocate you select should be someone you trust to name a competent successor.

> **Needed: common sense, generosity and good questions.**

If you are unable to identify an appropriate advocate, contact your local department of health or the local chapter of an advocacy group concerned with the beneficiary's disability. Often those organizations can provide good leads.

No matter whom you select, be sure to talk over your family situation with the advocate(s). Be frank. It's very important that they understand what they would be getting into. The more surprises they face, the greater the chance they will resign or, worse, do a lousy job. The better you prepare the advocate, the better your loved one will likely fare. For details on the sort of information you should collect for and share with the advocate, see Chapter 9.

Finally, consider again the issue of compensation. Your chosen advocate may well be someone who would not want to be paid, but you don't want to discourage them from taking an active role. Authorizing the trustee to pay the advocate's expenses can be a good investment.

Special Powers and Duties

Typical trust documents will include long lists of trustees' powers and duties. When reviewing a lawyer's draft, resist the temptation to skip over all that legal language. It may include things you don't want, and it may omit items which would be helpful in your situation.

For example, many trusts authorize the trustee to terminate the trust and distribute its

> **Personalize your trust.**

proceeds if the assets fall below a certain level. In many situations this power makes sense because it allows the trust to end before the administrative costs are so high they eat up all the income. As we'll see in the next chapter, however, a sudden influx of cash from a trust could disqualify a beneficiary from getting government assistance. If that is a concern, be sure the trustee will not distribute assets in a way that would endanger qualifying for government benefits.

On the other hand, there may be tasks you want to assign to your trustee (or advisor or advocate). Perhaps the trustee should visit the beneficiary every three or six months and should report to a local advocacy group about what was learned. Perhaps the advisor should interview the beneficiary before deciding whether to approve trust distributions. Perhaps the advocate should take the beneficiary to three baseball games each summer. Be creative: what sorts of things do you do now that you would like others to do in your absence? Put those directions into your trust.

Funding Your Trust

Your decisions about which assets to place in trust will depend upon several factors: the nature of those assets, their value, your beneficiaries' current and anticipated needs, who you choose as trustee, and the extent you want to maintain day-to-day control of assets.

One option is to use your will to create the trust, which would then be called a "testamentary trust." Your life insurance benefits could also be payable to the trust. To get into the trust, your assets (except the insurance money) would pass through probate, and the trust would continue to be supervised by the probate court.

Another choice is to create a trust which remains an empty shell designed to catch your assets at your death. Your will would direct that your estate be paid ("poured over") to the trust, and your life insurance could be payable to the trust. Again, your assets (except the insurance money) would pass through probate, but because you set up the trust before your death, the probate court would have no continuing supervisory power.

If avoiding probate is important, you could create a living trust by putting all your current assets in trust right away (see Chapter 2). If you want to maintain control, you could name yourself trustee and continue to manage the property. If you want independent management, you could name someone else (or a bank) to be trustee. In either case, your life insurance proceeds could be paid to the trust after your death.

> **What are your special assets?**

You may have special assets that call for special treatment. Many people provide that tangible personal property (the china cabinet, paintings, jewelry) be distributed to particular people or shared among a group. (Caution: if those assets are valuable, your gift could disqualify a beneficiary from getting government benefits.) Perhaps business assets should go in a separate trust with the managers acting as trustees. Perhaps your children would find it easier to share your vacation home or your boat if it were in trust for them. Talk with your advisor about special plans for those assets that are more than just investments.

Most families lack sufficient resources to provide for all of the needs of a disabled beneficiary. For them, private arrangements like trusts must dovetail with government assistance programs. Of particular concern is the danger of providing funds that disqualify the beneficiary from getting government help. Different considerations apply if you are creating a trust for someone else than if you are trying to qualify for Medicaid yourself. We now turn to those issues.

Questions to Consider

➤ Should I use a professional trustee? Who?

➤ Should I use a trust advisor? Who?

➤ What does the trustee fee cover?

➤ Does my disabled beneficiary need an advocate? Who?

➤ What special powers or duties fit my needs?

➤ What assets should I place in trust?

Chapter 5

Complementing Government Benefits

People who "plan while they can" commonly face a dilemma: they want to take care of a disabled person while at the same time preserving assets for others. When there isn't enough money to do both, one option is to plug into government benefit programs. The key here is to provide some help, but not so much as to disqualify the disabled person from getting government funds.

Because local eligibility rules vary considerably and change frequently, this chapter will not attempt to catalog specific requirements. You'll need to consult someone familiar with local practices in the place the disabled person lives. This chapter can help

Consult someone who knows local practices.

by describing the basic options available and identifying topics for you to consider as you seek advice.

Underlying almost all government support programs is one basic principle: claimants must show financial need. They may be disqualified if they have more assets or income than the maximum amounts set for various programs. The planning goal is to preserve as much wealth as possible without going over those maximum limits. Different rules apply depending upon whether you seek to help someone else who qualifies for benefits or whether you will be claiming benefits for yourself. First we'll cover how to make gifts for someone else without endangering their benefits. Then you'll learn what to consider if you believe you might qualify for benefits in the future, a topic typically called "Medicaid Planning."

Gifts to Others

In general, gifts to claimants will endanger their claims for benefits. Marc's experience shows how lack of planning can cause havoc. He was a single parent with two children, both young adults. His son, Michael, was disabled, working part time in a sheltered setting, and receiving government benefits. Marc's daughter, Karen, had a job at a local bookstore.

Some years ago, Marc's mother had purchased several U.S. Savings Bonds in her own name, but "Payable On Death" to each of her grandchildren. When she died, Michael and Karen split the proceeds. However, Michael lost his government assistance for two months because he had too many assets. He used up the Savings Bond money and had to re-apply for benefits.

When Marc died without a will two years later, Michael and Karen shared his estate equally. Michael again lost his benefits for a while and then had to qualify again. Three years later, Marc's brother died, leaving the proceeds of a life insurance policy "to my brother Marc, or if he predeceases me, equally to his children who survive me." Because Marc had died, Michael and Karen got the money. Michael lost his benefits again, this time for 8 months.

Marc's family could have preserved Michael's eligibility—and saved assets for use by others—by excluding Michael from their gift giving. In other words, they could have disinherited him. That solution sounds harsh, but may make good sense. If relatively smaller amounts of money are involved, excluding the disabled person may be the only practical way to avoid endangering that person's government benefits. (Of course, relying upon government assistance carries the risk that benefits will be cut or eliminated.) If you choose to disinherit someone for this reason, be sure to inform other family members so they don't make mistakes like Michael's grandmother and his uncle.

Many people—especially parents—are loath to disinherit

| **If you disinherit someone, explain why.** |

someone; they don't want that person to feel rejected. Of course, a severely mentally disabled person may be unaware of the situation and not be hurt. However, a great many disabled people—even those with severe mental retardation—would react with anger or disappointment upon learning they were left out. One solution is to discuss the situation ahead of time, so someone in Michael's shoes knows what to expect and why. If that isn't possible, a letter (or language in a will) can explain how much the person is loved even though left out.

If enough assets are available to justify establishing a trust, then more sophisticated planning is possible. We now turn to "Special Needs Trusts" you might create for someone else.

Special Needs Trusts

The basic idea of a special needs trust is to provide a source of funds to help a disabled beneficiary without disqualifying that person from receiving government benefits. For example, your daughter may really enjoy going to baseball games. In your absence, wouldn't it be nice for her to be able to afford an occasional game? A special needs trust can supply the funds to make that possible.

Rules vary from state to state, and local practices often vary from county to county. Sometimes statutes specifically authorize these trusts and set particular rules. Sometimes creative lawyers and clients have devised such trusts, and then courts have approved various features. Because there's so much variety, at least one member of your planning team should be familiar with the local rules of the place the disabled beneficiary will reside.

Special needs trusts can get their funds from a variety of sources. When there's been an accident, sometimes a court settlement provides the trust assets. Often parents or other family members set up special needs trusts for

> **Funds can come from many sources.**

disabled children. Such a trust can be an excellent solution for helping an unmarried partner. Life insurance frequently supplies all or most of the funding. Some statutes require the trust to be testamentary, so a will establishes the trust, which is funded from the probate estate (and perhaps life insurance).

If you create a durable power of attorney as described in Chapter 3, consider giving the power holder the additional authority to transfer funds to a special

> **"Pooled trusts" combine smaller funds.**

needs trust you are creating for someone else. Indeed, you may want to allow the power holder to set up such a trust on your behalf. Your trust document should refer to the durable power (and vice-versa) to make coordination easier.

People of modest means who want to establish special needs trusts may have trouble finding a trustee willing to administer relatively small amounts. To make such trusts more available, many states allow "pooled trusts" which combine the funds of many smaller special needs trusts. Pooling cuts down on the administrative costs, making these trusts more attractive to commercial banks. Pooled trusts usually must meet special rules.

Because a special needs trust is designed to complement government benefit programs, the trust should carefully state its purposes. Your lawyer should not rely on standard forms, but instead should work with you to identify what you are trying to accomplish. A purpose

> **Include a purpose statement tailored to you.**

statement tailored to your situation can both guide your trustee and help a court interpret the trust. At a minimum, it should make clear that the trust is intended to preserve the beneficiary's eligibility for government support by providing only for "special needs." You may also want to say that the primary purpose is providing for the disabled beneficiary, not those who would take what's left after the disabled person dies. You should avoid terms like "support" and "maintenance" because a court might focus on those and declare your trust appropriate to pay for expenses the government would otherwise cover.

Whether in the purpose statement or elsewhere, your trust should define the "special needs" of the disabled beneficiary. The basic theme should be needs beyond those the government support covers. If the disabled person has particular favorites—computers, backpacking, attending football games—mention those. Consider including medical and dental care which Medicaid will not cover. For example, Medicaid may deny a claim for a wheelchair until after a lengthy waiting period, but you may like to have one available immediately if it is needed.

As you decide on the basic structure of your trust, consider what other special powers or duties might fit your situation. You may want to require the trustee to seek government benefits, to accumulate any extra income, or to terminate the trust if the beneficiary meets a carefully-defined standard for living on her own. If you elect to name an advocate as discussed in Chapter 4, your purpose statement could mention paying the advocate's costs. One good idea is to allow the trustee to pay the provider of services or goods directly, rather than having to give funds to the beneficiary who then pays the bills.

> **Carefully consider who should get what's left.**

One of the most challenging questions is what to do with any funds that may be left after the disabled beneficiary dies. Some statutes allow special needs trusts, but only at the cost of reimbursing the state for all or some portion of the funds the state has spent on the beneficiary. Other states allow the balance to be paid to family members or friends. Be especially careful if you choose to give the balance to individuals who are serving in some capacity, such as trustee or trust advisor. You may not want to put the trustee or advisor in the position of having to take money out of their own (future) pocket in order to support the disabled beneficiary. One common solution is to designate a charity to receive any balance. This approach not only supports a worthy cause, but may also make a court more reluctant to rule that the trust fund must be exhausted before government benefits can become available.

So far, we have been talking about how to make gifts to others without endangering their benefits. Now we turn to what to consider if you believe you might qualify for benefits for yourself.

Medicaid Planning

Among our most common fears as we age is the prospect of spending our last few years in a nursing home while our savings shrink toward zero. Gener-

> **Medicaid: a last resort.**

ally aware of the Medicaid program, we wonder, "Could I give my property to my loved one and then let Medicaid pay for the nursing home?" The short, oversimplified answer is "No. Not unless you can anticipate when you'd need the nursing home and you are willing to live on meager resources for some time before you go into the nursing home." As a practical matter, Medicaid is a last resort.

On the other hand, people with modest resources who find themselves staring at nursing home expenses can plan in ways to minimize the effects on spouses and dependents. This section will briefly identify strategies for coping with the Medicaid rules. Although we talk in terms of Medicaid, the general principles we'll outline apply to a variety of government support programs.

First, consider the cost of gifts. The Medicaid rules are designed to keep you from making yourself suddenly poor so you can qualify for benefits. When you apply for benefits, the government will take a "snapshot" look at your financial situation at that time and will look back in time to see if you've given away property. With some narrow exceptions, if you've given property to others within the prior three years (five years for many gifts in trust), you will be subject to a penalty period during which you will be denied benefits.

Gifts can trigger penalty periods.

The length of the penalty period will depend upon the amount of your gift and the cost of nursing home care in your area. The basic idea is to treat you as if you had not given away the property by penalizing you for as long as you could have paid for your own care had you kept the property.

For example, suppose you gave your daughter property worth $30,000, and that a nursing home costs $3,000 per month. Your penalty period would be 10 months (30,000 divided by 3,000). After paying for your own care for those 10 months, you could qualify for benefits.

Notice that the "look back" periods—either 3 or 5 years, depending upon the situation—are not the same as the penalty periods. Assume you are applying for Medicaid today. You could have given your daughter a $3 million house 4 years ago and it wouldn't matter. The gift is beyond the look back period. On the other hand, if you had given her that same house 2 years ago, the gift would count, and your penalty period (assuming $3,000 per month costs) would be 1,000 months (just over 83 years)!

Despite the rules about gifts, Medicaid planning can be very important to many people. If you will face the necessity of applying for Medicaid, you can arrange your affairs to minimize

Many estate planners are not Medicaid experts.

the impact on the rest of your family. Be sure to consult someone who regularly works with the Medicaid rules. Many excellent estate planners know very little about Medicaid, so be careful.

A big part of Medicaid planning involves using the program's exemptions to the best advantage. In particular, you may be able to move funds from "countable" resources to "exempt" resources. Money in a savings account (above a minimum amount) would keep you from qualifying. But if you spend that

money on

| **Shift from countable to exempt resources.** |

an exempt resource, you can in some sense keep it in the family. For example, your state may not count a van as a resource which would keep you from qualifying for benefits. As you "spend down" your assets to approach the qualification levels, you might want to invest in a nice van with a lift and adaptive equipment inside. Similarly, because houses are exempt resources, you may want to put a new roof on your house or add a bedroom. These adjustments—before applying for Medicaid—can make life a bit easier for your dependents.

In general, the technique of shifting assets to exempt resources serves to buy time. In the long run, states are supposed to pursue claims for Medicaid reimbursement against your estate (or the estate of your surviving spouse once that person dies). Enforcement is a bit uneven, but it is becoming more and more difficult to claim Medicaid benefits for yourself and still leave substantial assets to your family and friends.

Because Medicaid is not designed to meet the needs of most Americans, many people are taking a closer look at long-term care insurance, the subject of Chapter 6.

Questions to Consider

➢ Is disinheritance a good option?

➢ What versions of a special needs trust are available locally?

➢ Who should get what's left over?

➢ Is Medicaid planning appropriate for me?

Chapter 6

Long Term Care Insurance

Disabled people often need help with activities of daily living—bathing, dressing, cooking, cleaning, and the rest. Friends or relatives may lend a hand occasionally or even regularly, but some of us don't have that kind of help available or eventually the burden just becomes too great. Then the need arises to hire someone or to move to a facility, perhaps a nursing home, which can provide such services. The questions become: What will that cost and how can I pay for it?

The cost, of course, will vary in different areas of the country and will depend upon the level and quality of the services provided. By way of comparison, it may help to know that nursing home costs nationally now average between $40,000 and $50,000 per year. Because these are national averages, you should check out the costs in the area you expect to be living.

The average nursing home resident stays about 2 1/2 years, though not necessarily all at once. As a ballpark estimate, that means national average costs run between $100,000 and $150,000, without any cushion in case extra expenses come up or a longer stay is required. Keep in mind that these estimates are in current dollars. Over time, inflation is almost certainly going to increase these costs. For example, if costs increase six percent annually, today's $40,000 expense would cost over $67,500 in 10 years.

What's the best way to cover such expenses? Many people simply believe (or hope) they'll never need extended care. Others decide they can "self-insure" by relying upon their savings, investments, life insurance, and the equity in their homes to cover the cost. In the past few years long-term care insurance has become an increasingly popular option. Deciding whether to invest in long-term care insurance and what policy to buy can be a daunting task. This chapter can help by providing a method for evaluating your options. The more familiar you are with the questions you'll face, the better you will be able to work with your advisors to select the best choice for you.

A Comparison Chart

One way to organize the relevant information is to make a comparison chart. Your chart might look something like the example on the next page:

	Policy 1	Policy 2	Policy 3	Policy 4
Item 1				
Item 2				
Item 3				

Across the top you would list the various policies you are considering. Down the left side, enter the different questions you have about the policies. For a starting place, consider the points raised below. Then add items that fit your particular situation. You may also want to consult with your advisor about other topics to consider. Next, fill in the blanks with the help of your advisor. Be careful, however, not to rely upon an insurance agent's word about policy features; be sure you find appropriate provisions written into the policy. When you are finished, you will have assembled a great deal of information in a summary form.

To evaluate that information, review the chart box-by-box and put a "+" sign in boxes which describe favorable features and a "–" sign in boxes which identify negative features. Then, tally up each policy, noting which ones offer more of what you want and less of what you don't like or need. Finally, evaluate whether the benefits are worth the costs in light of your family's resources and general health.

Creating Your Chart

What follows is a starting place for developing a chart that suits your needs. You will want to refine this list when you consult your advisors. Put questions like these in the left hand column of your chart.

What is the premium? With most policies, you will have to wait to fill in this information until after you have selected among some of the choices noted below. However, putting it at the top of the list underscores an important point: if you can't afford (or don't want to pay) the premium, don't buy the policy. Unfortunately, many people sign up for long-term care insurance and then drop their policies when the cost actually hits home. Basically, they have wasted their money.

Is there a spousal discount? Some policies offer lower premiums to married people, especially if each purchases a policy.

Is there a waiver of premium provision? These provide that once benefits begin, you no longer continue to pay premiums. Some policies provide a premium waiver for a surviving spouse after the other spouse dies.

Is there a return of premium provision? Some policies will return some or all of the premiums you pay if you don't end up needing the insurance. Of course, the company will have your money in the meantime and will be paying you back in dollars made less valuable (at least to some extent) by inflation.

Is the policy guaranteed to be renewable? If your health takes a turn for the worse, you would not want to lose your coverage.

What circumstances will trigger coverage? Most policies pay benefits after the insured person cannot perform some number of "activities of daily living," like bathing, dressing, moving around, and eating. Because different policies define these activities in different ways, carefully compare the language.

Are pre-existing conditions covered? Many people with existing disabilities or checkered health histories are still able to get insurance, though often at a higher rate.

The key here is disclosure. If you know of a condition, be sure to include that information on your application form. Trying to hide something now will likely cause the insurance company to deny coverage later. You might want to fill out the form and then ask your family doctor to review it for things you might have left out.

Are there any other exclusions? Check carefully to see if particular conditions—especially ones that concern you—are excluded from coverage.

What is the benefit amount? The highest benefit may not be best for you. By selecting a lower benefit, you may be able to keep the policy's premium down. Of course, that approach will also mean that if you do need care, you'll have to come up with the difference between the policy's benefit and the actual cost of care.

Is the benefit amount indexed for inflation? The tendency of health care costs to rise, sometimes very rapidly, makes inflation coverage attractive. On the other hand, it may be costly. Again, the question is how much you want to pay now to avoid the risk of facing higher expenses later.

How is inflation protection figured? Different policies may use different formulas for computing the rate of inflation. They may cap the amount of increase at a particular percentage, either each year or in total over the length of the policy. They may not reflect compounded increases (those which build upon the increases of each prior year).

Is the benefit amount set on a daily or a monthly basis? A monthly cap can provide greater flexibility, but may cost more.

Does the plan pay a set amount (indemnity) period or does it pay for actual charges (reimbursement) up to a cap? Indemnity plans may return your premium dollars faster, but may cost more.

How soon will coverage begin after services are used? Policies typically provide a "waiting period" which serves rather like a deductible for an auto insurance policy. You may be able to save substantially on your insurance premium by being will-ing to foot the bill yourself for the first several days of care.

What is covered? You'll need several boxes for this one, depending upon your anticipated needs. Here's a preliminary list:

- Rehabilitation facilities
- Intermediate care facilities
- Visiting nurses
- Occupational Therapy
- Physical Therapy
- Speech Therapy
- Psychology services
- Dental care
- Homemaker services
- Care-advisory services

- Prescription drugs
- Medical supplies, equipment and home modification

Some policies add extra charges (or additional deductibles) for some items, and some don't cover them at all. As you compare the coverage different policies provide, keep in mind that your budget should include anticipated costs for those expenses not covered by any particular policy.

To what extent are benefits subject to income tax? Tax rules are known to change often, so it is wise to get current advice on whether the benefits paid under a particular policy will be treated as taxable income to you if those benefits are paid.

Questions to Consider

➢ Should I "self-insure" from my savings or buy a long-term care policy?

➢ If I do buy a policy, what combination of costs and benefits best suits my situation?

Section III

Life and Death Decisions

Life and Death Decisions

This section addresses the difficult and emotionally-charged questions of how health care decisions—especially end-of-life decisions—are made for people who lack the capacity to choose for themselves. Basically, the law provides three, sometimes overlapping options for how to handle this situation:

- **Living Will.** If the patient has left a set of instructions – popularly called a "living will"—those directions may be able to guide the decision.

- **Surrogate by Statute.** Many state statutes provide a preference list for appointing a surrogate decisionmaker to decide on behalf of the incapacitated patient. These apply if the patient has not named someone who can serve that function. Typically the list does **not** include non-relatives.

- **Health Care Proxy.** Many state statutes allow individuals to appoint their own surrogate decisionmakers by creating a special document. The most common term for these documents is "durable power of attorney for

health care," but the label "health care proxy"
is starting to catch on.

Planning for future health care presents two related problems. First is the need to figure out, as best you can, both how you would like to be treated in common situations and, perhaps more importantly, what your philosophy will be for facing death. Second is finding the means to communicate those wishes to others. The next chapter offers suggestions for thinking through the hard questions. Then we turn to details of the legal documents—called "advance directives"—you can use to increase the chances that your wishes will be followed.

Chapter 7

Hard Choices

Whether you are preparing a living will or plan to complete a health care proxy (or both), you should spend some time thinking about what care you would want in different situations. A simple, single rule won't work for most of us. Consider the feeding tubes used to deliver nutrition if we can't eat. We might want them in the first couple of days after a serious accident, but not want them keeping us alive for months in a coma. This chapter can help you and those you love come to grips with the hard choices we all may face.

The first step is to recognize that for most of us, these decisions take time. Quickly checking a few boxes on a living will form in a lawyer's office or a hospital waiting room is not the best approach. Give yourself a chance to reflect on your initial reactions.

As a guide to working through these issues, you might want to start by asking yourself some general questions to identify your views. Here's a start:

- What gives meaning and purpose to my life?

- What are my religious or spiritual beliefs about death?
- What are my goals for my future?
- How important is it to leave an estate for my family?
- How important is my personal mobility?
- How much do I value my ability to do things on my own?
- Would I rather be alert and in pain, or sedated and more comfortable?
- How much is death something to be postponed?

Use this list to help trigger your thinking about other related topics important to you.

Next, write down your answers in some form. You might simply write a few sentences in response to each question. You might write up a letter to loved ones discussing these issues. Writing down your answers may be difficult, but it is an important step. The act of putting your thoughts into words on paper will help you become more specific. Just as importantly, others will have a good way of knowing your wishes should the need arise. If writing is too difficult, put your thoughts on tape.

With those general ideas in mind, turn your attention to more specific issues. We can't really anticipate what life will bring. By comparing our reactions to different possible situations, however, we can develop some guidelines that can help when real problems arise. A chart like this can help:

Across the top row sketch in a series of possible situations you might face. Your own medical and family histories will be your best guide, but here are a few suggestions:

- Good chance of surviving. Probable speech (or mobility) disability.
- Poor chance of surviving. Probable speech (or mobility) disability.
- Good chance of surviving. Probable substantial difficulty thinking.
- Good chance of surviving this procedure, but terminally ill. Probable substantial difficulty thinking.

Down the left column list common medical treatments, again drawing upon your own experience. Your list might include:

- Nutrition (food tubes)
- Hydration (water by iv or food tube)
- Pain medication
- Antibiotics
- Blood transfusions
- Chemotherapy
- Simple tests (X-rays, blood tests)
- Invasive tests (tubes searching internal organs)
- Respirator
- Artificial heart pump
- Kidney dialysis

For each situation, work down the list and write "yes" or "no" in the boxes. Finally, make a few copies of your completed chart.

Having thought carefully about some health care choices, you are ready to consider how best to insure that your wishes will be honored. That is the subject of the next chapter.

Questions to Consider

➢ What are my feelings about health and disability?

➢ What treatments would I want in different situations?

➢ What treatments would I reject?

Chapter 8

Advance Directives

Armed with some specific ideas about health care alternatives, you face the question of how best to communicate your views to those who may be making decisions about your care. In most states, you may choose one or both forms of advance directives: living wills and health care proxies (durable powers for health care). You may want to review Chapter 2's introduction to these devices.

Typically, living wills cover only terminal illnesses. Some states similarly restrict proxies, while other states recognize the advantage of allowing them to apply in a broad range of circumstances. This chapter can help you decide whether and how to use these legal tools.

Living Wills

Living wills give directions to others on what health care you would like to receive if you

Living wills speak for you.

have a terminal illness and are unable to communicate. One way to think about them is that they speak for you when you cannot speak for yourself, in contrast to health care proxies, which name another person to speak for you. By the way, be careful with the term "living will." You may hear people using "living will" when they mean "advance directive," without distinguishing between the two types. You may have to ask them whether they mean a living will or a health care proxy (durable power).

Though there have been efforts to get states to agree on a single, national form, most states have their own slightly different rules about what a living will can cover and what it takes to make it effective. To be safe, you should use the form of your home state. (If you spend extended periods in a different state, you might want to complete that state's form as well and keep it with you when you are there.)

Many living will forms include lots of details identifying different possible treatments, usually giving the direction that you do not want the treatment listed. Read the form carefully to be sure you agree with what it says. Because the living will in theory speaks for you, in most cases it will control your care, even if family members say you would not want that result.

If you don't know some of the terms used, ask a health care professional. Especially watch the term "terminal illness." Usually the living will won't apply unless you have a terminal illness. Sometimes the form will define the term, some-

What's a "terminal illness"?

98

times not. Because "terminal" may mean different things to different people, you may want to speak with your physician about the approach he or she would take in deciding whether you had a terminal illness.

Living wills usually are not "take it or leave it" documents. You can scratch out terms you don't like. Often you'll be able to check or initial various boxes to indicate your choices. In particular, many forms ask separately for your views on whether you would like nutrition (food tubes) or hydration (water). The chart described in Chapter 7 should help you as you review your form.

Health Care Proxy

A Health Care Proxy—also known as a Durable Power for Health Care—gives other people the authority to decide what health care you should receive if you are unable to communicate. Legally, such documents are a lot like the durable powers for financial planning, discussed in Chapter 3. Sometimes they are even combined in the same power of attorney. You'll recall that a power of attorney is a document through which you authorize someone to act on your behalf while you are alive. Because confusion can result from these different uses, many people (and this book) use the term "health care proxy" when only health care decisions are involved.

Some states limit the use of health care proxies to situations involving a terminal illness; other states recognize them any time the principal is unable to express his or her wishes. In either case, creating an effective proxy involves two important steps: choosing the agent and informing the agent.

Give careful thought to choosing your agent and—if possible—an alternate in case your first choice is unavailable. Your agent should be someone who is levelheaded in a crisis and who will follow **your** wishes, not their own. Many of us choose close family members because we know them, and they know us, so well. That approach might not always be wise. Because they are close to you, the pressure of your medical crisis may cloud their thinking. Because their personal lives will be shaped by their decisions, they may be tempted to do what *they* would like, rather than what *you* would like. As always when choosing someone to act for you, pick carefully.

> **Choose someone who will honor your wishes.**

Another consideration is distance. When possible, health care decisions should be made by people on the scene. They can talk with health care providers face-to-face. They can see you and gauge your condition. If you have more than one equally qualified candidate, perhaps your first choice should be the one who can be with you in the shortest (and stay for the longest) time.

Once you have identified an agent, be sure to communi-

| Have a frank discussion. |

cate your wishes to your agent.
Much too often, we simply as-
sume that those close to us know what we think, even when
they aren't sure. A good way to inform your agent is to discuss
with the agent the topics you covered while working out your
own choices with the help of Chapter 7. If you prepared a chart
or other paperwork, give the agent a copy. In any case, be sure
to have a frank conversation about life and death issues with
your agent <u>and</u> with any alternates.

Living Will or Health Care Proxy?

Because most states recognize both living wills and
health care proxies, you may have to decide which approach to
take, or whether to create both kinds of documents. In some
ways the advantages of each option mirrors the disadvantages of
the other.

Because living wills speak for you and contain specific instructions, they provide some security that your wishes will be
honored. If you create both a living will and a health care proxy,
and if the living will covers the situation that arises, health care
providers usually will favor the living will over conflicting advice from someone holding a proxy. As long as you are confident
that the living will reflects your desires, that is a good thing.

With medicine producing new treatments all the time, keeping current can be a problem.

Another advantage of living wills is that they protect people who are isolated from friends and relatives. For people who are alone, a proxy is of no help.

On the other hand, if you do have support from people you trust, a health care proxy offers the kind of flexibility that a living will can't. Health care often presents ambiguous situations, ones not as clear-cut as we would like. Your living will may not cover the precise problem you face. Someone armed with a proxy—and with the knowledge of how you approach health care issues—can have the flexibility to work out a solution close to what you would have chosen.

Because some people fear giving too much power to someone else, most states allow a health care proxy to act in some ways like a living will. If you want to cover specific situations, you can direct your agent on how to handle them. You might cover a particular illness or treatment. You might make clear the agent has a particular power, like removing you from a hospital or nursing home. You can also withhold the agent's power to decide particular issues. Of course, that will only insure that if the agent doesn't decide, someone else will.

The principal advantage of health care proxies is that they preserve flexibility in the face of our changing health-care scene. They are especially useful devices in states that recognize them in a broad range of situations, rather than only in terminal cases. On the other hand, proxies are only as good as the people who exercise them.

Spreading the Word

In the real world of health care decisions, advance directives often get ignored. Often the people making the decisions—the physicians, the emergency room nurses, the paramedics—don't know of the advance directive or don't have time to consult either a document or a person. One way to combat this problem is to let many people know what you have decided.

If you involve your family physician from the start, he or she is more likely to remember that you care about these issues. Ask their advice:

- How reliable are estimates of survival?
- What does "terminal" mean?
- How easy would it be for me to become dependent upon a respirator?
- Are there any developing treatments I should know about?

When you have completed your documents, be sure your primary care physician has an original version (including the background material described in the last chapter). In many states, a copy will serve as an original.

Getting your documents into a file in your doctor's office may not be enough. If you have a file at a local hospital, add your advance directives to that. Of course, if you create a health care proxy, be sure your agent (and any alternates) has copies. You might also want to share your documents with a variety of family members, just so they know what you've done in case they are called upon.

Questions to Consider

➢ Do I want a Living Will?

➢ What should it say about specific treatments?

➢ Do I want a Health Care Proxy?

➢ Whom should I name?

➢ Should I limit the power in any ways?

➢ Have I notified others about the documents I've prepared?

Section IV

Teamwork

Teamwork

Because you are familiar with the basic tools and have considered how those devices can be shaped to help your situation, you are well prepared to put all your planning to work for you. The key concept for translating these ideas into practical solutions is teamwork. It seldom makes sense to face such important and complex decisions on your own. This section offers practical suggestions on assembling and organizing your own files, choosing your team of advisors, and working with them to produce the best possible plan.

Chapter 9

Getting It Together

Before setting out to select and meet with advisors, review your personal files to be sure they are current and organized in a way that will allow you to use them easily throughout the planning process. As you work through this chapter, keep in mind that there is no magic "best" system. A system is good if it works for those who have to use it. In this case, that means you and those who might need to find something in your absence.

A filing system will work well if there are neither too many nor too few divisions. Too many categories makes it likely that you (or someone else) will put something in the "wrong" file and be unable later to remember where it is. Too few categories means thick files that force you to look through lots of papers to find the one you need. In any case, you can always adjust your system over time, combining small files and subdividing large ones as your needs change.

The first step is to identify major categories. Here are some possibilities:

- Education
- Employment
- Estate Planning
- Financial
- Medical
- Personal

In most families, each of these topics would need several sub-files, but by grouping them this way it should be easier to find a series of related files at once. You might want to color code the main categories. For example, all education files might be in blue folders, or have blue dots on the tabs. The categories are in alphabetical order, and within each category the sub-files follow that pattern.

Each file's tab would show both the general category and the sub-file titles. (You may have to abbreviate.) That way you'll know exactly where to replace the file when you are finished using it. A typical file tab might look like these:

```
Education - Rick -
```

```
┌─────────────────────────────────────┐
│  Financial - Bank -                 │
└─────────────────────────────────────┘
```

Below is an illustrative file system for an imaginary family. Suppose Ray and Dorothy are in their 40's. They have two school-age children: Melody and Rick. Dorothy was recently diagnosed with Multiple Sclerosis. Rick suffered brain damage in an auto accident. They have a separate file for each item listed below. (If the file only shows a name, it includes everything in that category for that person.)

Education –

　　Melody

　　Rick – Grade Reports

　　Rick – Individual Education Plans

Employment –

　　Dorothy

　　Ray – Jefferson High School

　　Ray – House Painters, Inc.

Estate Planning –

　　Basic Info

　　Powers of Attorney

　　Rick's Needs

　　Wills

Financial –

    Bank – Checking

    Bank – Savings

    Debts – Auto Loan

    Debts – Master Card

    Debts – Mortgage

    Debts – Visa

    Insurance – Auto

    Insurance – Health – Claims Pending

    Insurance – Health – Policy

    Insurance – Life – Melody – MONY

    Insurance – Life – Melody – Prudential

    Insurance – Life – Rick – NW Mutual

    Investments– Certificates of Deposit – First Bank

    Investments – Certificates of Deposit – Second
        Bank

    Investments – Mutual Funds – Fidelity

    Investments – Mutual Funds – Vanguard

    Real Estate – 1602 Birch Lane

    Real Estate – Clear Lake Cabin

Taxes – Income [by year] –

Taxes – Real Estate

Medical –

Dorothy – Health Care Proxy

Dorothy – Tests

Dorothy –Therapy

Ray – General

Ray – Health Care Proxy

Rick – Tests

Rick – Therapy

Rick – Surgeries

Melody

Two of the files noted above require some more explanation. Both are sub-categories of Estate Planning. The "Basic Info" file collects information that would be of a great help to someone handling an estate. It might include:

- Phone numbers for those to contact in an emergency: relatives, clergy, employers, and volunteer organizations.

- Names, birth dates, Social Security numbers, marital histories, and addresses for each family member.

- Names and phone numbers for everyone on your planning team.

- Location of wills and similar documents

- Bank and brokerage account and phone numbers

- Location of safe deposit box

- Locations of family heirlooms

- Special requests regarding funeral and burial arrangements.

The "Rick's Needs" file is different from the others and took a good deal of preparation. Its purpose is to provide background information for anyone having to care for Rick in the future. Guidance like this would be especially useful to the advocate described in Chapter 4 or to a guardian. This is also the kind of information you should share with your team when you meet to develop your plan. A "needs" file might include:

- **Identifying data**: nickname, Social Security number, phone numbers, clothing sizes, birth date

- **Important people** (and addresses for each): parents, siblings, spouse, children, friends, clergy, guardian, trustee, agent under a power of attorney
- **Religion**: membership, level of involvement
- **Education**: past and current schooling, interests, nature of any additional services (speech, occupational therapy)
- **Medical information**: physical condition (be specific), past and current doctors and dentists, diagnoses, blood type, immunizations, hospitalizations, birth control, medications (prescription and over-the-counter), adaptive or prosthetic devices
- **Daily care**: typical schedule, level of independence at various tasks (bathing, dressing, cooking, shopping, housekeeping), food likes and dislikes, favorite personal hygiene products, special problem areas (and approaches) [To put this together, you might try keeping notes for a week on a pad kept in a convenient place.]
- **Housing**: history, suggestions for the future

- **Financial**: allowance, ability to budget, sources of funds, typical expenses
- **Employment**: job history, assessment of strengths and weaknesses
- **Recreation**: interests, habits, vacation history

When you have an up-to-date set of information, you are ready to select a team. That's the topic of the next chapter.

Questions to Consider

➢ What categories of information do I need?

➢ Which topics are worth their own files?

➢ Would a "needs" file help?

Chapter 10

Choosing Your Advisors

Selecting an advisory team from among different groups of professionals can be a daunting task, especially when some of them are clamoring for your business and others seem hidden in the shadows. Many of us are tempted to shorten the process by hiring a friend of a friend, and letting it go at that. Consider for a moment how much effort you put into selecting a new car or even a washing machine. Comparing features and cost seems almost second nature. Aren't the plans for your future, or that of someone you love, just as important? Adopting a three-step approach can ease the process. First, build a list of potential team members. Second, interview likely candidates. Third, evaluate those you've seen.

Build a List

Building a list involves two different phases. First, identify the various areas of expertise that bear on your situation. Next, identify particular individuals who might be able to help you in each of those areas.

Areas of interest. When you look carefully at your needs, you'll probably discover that you will want to consult some of these professionals:

- A lawyer with expertise in disability planning
- An insurance advisor (or more): life, health, disability, long-term care
- A financial planner
- An accountant
- A bank trust officer
- A social worker
- A geriatric/disability care manager
- A health care provider (or more): nurse, occu-pational therapist, physical therapist, primary care physician, specialist.

Identifying individuals. To fill in names for various categories, you can draw upon a number of sources for recommendations:

- Family members and friends, remembering that their needs may be different from yours

- Religious advisors, remembering that a member of your congregation may not have the expertise you need
- Professionals you already know, remembering that their own self-interest may cloud their judgment about who would be best for you
- Local support groups for various disabilities
- Directories of professional organizations, taking advantage of indexes or sections which group people by specialty
- The Internet, through web sites of professional organizations or sites (called "portals") that collect links to several sites about a common topic.
- The phone book, using display ads to gain information, but taking them with a grain (or more) of salt

Interview Your Candidates

Once you have your list of names, the next step is to pick the 2 or 3 most attractive candidates in each category. The more important the role of a particular

We learn by comparisons.

team member, the more you should take special care in your selection. Resist the temptation to see only one. Often we can learn much by comparisons. While interviewing a second person, we see better what we liked and disliked about the first (and vice-versa).

Call the people on your "short list," and make appointments to speak with them. Tell them your purpose: you want to decide whether to hire them. The appointment should be short (about a half hour) and free.

At the interview, you'll need to sketch the basic facts of your situation, so your potential team member can discuss how he or she would approach the project. Beware of the temptation to get bogged down in details. For example, tell a lawyer that you want to consider creating a trust, but don't add that you are debating among 3 possible trustees. Remember that the purpose of this meeting is to decide about hiring the advisor, not to do the actual planning.

Here are some questions to ask during the interview. Be sure to take notes about both the answers and your reactions to them.

- Please describe your practice. What kinds of problems do you address? How much of your time involves disability planning (or care)? Why are you doing this sort of work?

- Would you be doing the actual work on my project, or would some junior member of your organization handle it? With whom would I (or my disabled family member) be working?

- How would we communicate? This question is especially important if geography separates team members from each other, you, or the disabled person. It also gives you a chance to see how open the person is to communicating at all.

- What would be your anticipated fees? How would they be calculated?

Assess Your Candidates

While each meeting is still fresh in your mind, jot down some notes about it. When you have interviewed the candidates in each category, compare your notes and decide whom to hire. Questions like these will help your evaluation:

- How do I feel about this person? Liking a professional advisor, or even a care worker, as a friend is not necessary. On the other hand, if you dislike someone, you should look further. Dislike easily turns to distrust, which destroys the relationship you are trying to build. Moreover, you will probably tend to avoid contacting someone you dislike. Why hire someone you'd later want to avoid?

- Did the person know what he or she was talking about? Could they communicate in terms I could understand?

- Did this person listen – really listen – to me? Was I treated as an individual? Would I get "cookie-cutter" treatment like others on an assembly line, or attention tailored to my needs? Will he or she be able to see the world through my eyes?

- Would the gender, race, age, ethnic background, or economic status of the person affect our relationship?

- What were the surroundings like? Was the office so scruffy that I wondered if it would be in business very long? Was the office so disorganized that I feared my files would get lost? Was the office so fancy that I feared over-charging? Would the office be accessible to a disabled client?

- How well would this person be able to work with other members of my advisory team?

When you have assembled your team, the time has come to work together developing and implementing your plan. That's the subject of our final chapter.

Questions to Consider

➤ What categories of information do I need?

➤ Have I consulted several sources for my list of team candidates?

➤ Have I prepared for the hiring interviews?

➤ Do I have confidence in my team?

Chapter 11

Working Together

You've updated your files and selected your advisory team. Now it's time to design and implement a plan that meets your needs. For most people – especially those facing disability – this process will take time. Instant solutions lack the substance of those that take longer to prepare. Moreover, it is a process that probably will need repeating, as your situation changes over time. This chapter offers ways to handle each stage of the process, from initial meetings, through conferences, to periodic reviews.

Initial Planning Meetings

Your first meeting (after the hiring interview) with each advisor is critically important. You will have already started to establish a relationship, but here is

> **Come prepared.**

where you will really begin to build mutual trust. It's just as important that the advisor trust you, as it is that you trust the advisor. Come to your meeting prepared, ready to share both information and ideas.

125

Review your files (and portions of this book) before your meeting. You'll need somewhat different information for different advisors. Lawyers will be more interested in financial information; health care workers will want medical histories. When you make your appointment, ask what sort of information to bring. But don't let the advisors operate in their own little pigeonholes. Building a *team* approach will require each of them to become informed about other aspects of your situation. For example, be sure the lawyer knows some details about the medical condition of a disabled family member.

The most important thing to bring to the meeting is an open attitude. You've chosen people you can trust. Trust them. Be candid; glossing over problems only hurts in the long run. Share your needs, your fears, your hopes.

| **Be candid.** |

Sharing can be scary, but remember that the better they know you (and your family), the better advice you'll get. Take advantage of their duty to keep your affairs confidential.

Be ready – and willing – to ask questions and make suggestions. This book has put you in the position to do just that. You may have to push your advisor a bit. Some will not be expecting a client as well prepared as you will be. Be persistent, and they'll get the idea. Develop a real conversation, one that moves both directions. Build upon your advisor's thoughts by

126

offering refinements that meet your needs. Suggest your own ideas, while staying open to refinements your advisor may suggest. Take notes. By the end of your first (or maybe second) meeting, your advisor should have a pretty good feel for your needs and the potential solutions that appeal to you.

The next step is to ask for a proposal. Many lawyers will want to move directly to a set of documents for you to review.

| **Get proposals.** | Insurance agents will want to prepare policies. Investment advisors will want you to |

invest. Resist that approach at this stage. What you need right now is something you can share with other team members: a *description* of the *plan*.

As you meet with different advisors, keep one question in the back of your mind. Who would be best suited to lead the team? Who has the background and the skill to communicate with everyone and pull the plan together? In most situations, the best team leader will be you. Don't be reluctant to take charge. It is, after all, *your* plan. Of course, you may need someone else to lead the team, or you may want to groom someone to take on that role when you can't. If so, carefully consider people with whom you've had long-standing relationships. They are more likely to understand your situation better and to follow through.

When you've educated your advisors and settled on a leader, you're ready for the team meeting.

The Team Meeting

The size and scope of your team meeting will depend upon your situation. Health care professionals and social workers will be important if you are planning for someone who currently has a disability. They wouldn't be needed if you are anticipating the possibility of a future disability. An accountant may not be needed if your financial situation is not complicated. However, most meetings will call for a lawyer, insurance agents, and a financial advisor.

You may meet some resistance to a team meeting. A team approach to planning is relatively rare. Professionals are busy and hard to get together. Besides, each feels more comfortable

> **A brainstorming session.**

in their own environment, where they don't have to consider other aspects of your situation. Make the extra effort to bring as many as possible together. Having broken the ice, you'll make it easier for them to consult each other. Most importantly, you'll have their collective ideas as you settle on a plan.

In the ideal world, each of your advisors will have prepared a written proposal you can then share with the others. They'll come to a meeting having reviewed each other's ideas, ready to make and respond to suggestions. Rather than being defensive about advancing their own ideas, they'll be looking forward to brainstorming together. You'll leave with a complete set of notes covering all aspects of your plan.

Of course, we don't live in an ideal world. It won't work that smoothly. But you can expect to get everyone to see the big picture, not just their own little corner. You can expect some new ideas to emerge. Most importantly, you should be able to develop a plan that moves in one direction, instead of pulling against itself.

Implementing the Plan

Once you have worked out a plan, you can implement it. Now is the time start your investment plan. Review wills, trusts, powers of attorney,

| Review documents carefully. |

and insurance policies. Be careful, however. Be sure that the legal documents really do reflect the decisions you've made. Be skeptical. Professionals (especially lawyers) work from forms, so you may find some things you haven't discussed, and there may be some things missing. Keep asking questions. Insist on **your** plan. Then sign the appropriate documents and feel the satisfaction that comes from doing an important job well.

Making Adjustments

Enjoy your success, but don't rest on your laurels. Life goes on, and plans often need to change. When your situation—health, finances, family—changes, it's time to touch base with the team. Maybe a few phone calls will be enough. Maybe you'll need another meeting, perhaps with new advisors. Because you've been an active, informed participant in the planning process, changes should be easier to design and implement.

Best Wishes

Having established a plan that fits your unique needs, you will have created some peace of mind for yourself and those you love. Best wishes!

Questions to Consider

➢ What do I need to bring to my first planning meeting?

➢ Who should lead the team?

➢ Who will I need at the team meeting?

➢ Does my new situation call for another meeting?

INDEX

ABOUT THE AUTHOR

Roger W. Andersen is a Professor of Law at the University of Toledo. He is the author of two books used in law schools, in addition to numerous articles for professional and lay audiences. Professor Andersen has taught Trusts and Estates for 25 years and also offered courses in Elder Law and Disability Law. He has law degrees from the University of Iowa and the University of Illinois. Prior to entering teaching, he did estate planning in a trust department and in private law practice. His interest in Elder Law and disability issues stems from his personal experience helping relatives and friends plan to face the challenges of aging or disability.